Key Stage 1

English Revision Guide

Carol Matchett

Schofield & Sims

Welcome to this book

This book will help you revise what you have learnt in Years 1 and 2.

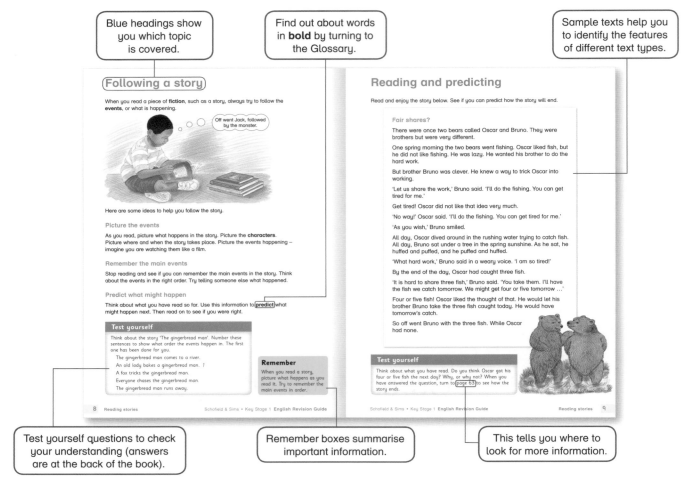

Blue headings show you which topic is covered.

Find out about words in **bold** by turning to the Glossary.

Sample texts help you to identify the features of different text types.

Test yourself questions to check your understanding (answers are at the back of the book).

Remember boxes summarise important information.

This tells you where to look for more information.

How to revise

- Turn to the topic and read about it.

- Read the Remember box and then cover it up. Can you remember what it says?

- Read the Test yourself questions and write your answers on a piece of paper.

- Check your answers against the right answers at the back of the book.

- If you got any answers wrong, read the topic again, then have another go at the questions.

- If you got the answers right – well done! Move on to the next topic.

- Once you have worked through this revision guide, move on to the **Key Stage 1 English Practice Papers**.

Tips for tests

- Always read the question carefully before you answer it.

- Have a go at as many questions as you can. If there is a question you really can't answer, just move on to the next one. You can always come back to it if you have time.

- Look out for questions that ask you to explain. This means that you must give reasons.

- If you have time at the end, check through your work.

Contents

Reading difficult words

When you are reading, you might sometimes come to a word you do not know. Use your word reading skills to help you quickly work out the word.

Use phonics

Say the sounds that go with the letters. **Blend** the sounds together so you can hear the word.

s … c … r … ee … ch   ⟵ makes 'screech'

Try different sounds

Some letters have more than one sound. Sometimes you blend a word but it does not sound right. Try a different sound. The **sentence** around it will help you.

w-i-l-d   She was wild…   ⟵ i makes a 'long i' sound in this word

Look for syllables

If the word is long, break it up into smaller parts or **syllables**. Each syllable is a beat of the word. Read each syllable and then put the word together.

sud-den-ly   ⟵ makes 'suddenly'

Look for words and suffixes

You might see a word you know and then a **suffix** on the end. Build the word up.

excite + ment   ⟵ makes 'excitement'

Go back and check

When you think you know the word, go back to the start of the sentence. Read the sentence again. Check the word makes sense in the sentence.

Suddenly, the screech of an owl woke Poppy. She was wild with excitement.

Test yourself

1. Use your word reading skills to read these words. (They are all real words.)

stupid shriek wander amusement rudely envelope

Remember

Make use of your word reading skills. Sound out any difficult words.

Reading for meaning

Reading is not just about reading the words on a page. Reading is about making sense of the words and following the meaning.

Here are two things to remember to help you read for meaning.

Read aloud in your head

'Listen' to what you are reading so you can hear the meaning.

The third little pig built a house. The house was made of bricks.

Check that it makes sense

Everything you read should make sense. If it makes sense you have probably read it correctly.

If something does not make sense, then stop, go back and re-read.

1. Stop reading.

2. Go back to the start of the sentence.

3. Read it again. Find the word that did not make sense. See if you can work it out.

4. Read the whole sentence with the right word and meaning.

Test yourself

Read these sentences aloud in your head. Find the word that does not make sense. Can you work out what the word should be?

1. All the word was now in darkness.

2. The frog started at the silver moon.

3. On the place steps stood Queen Beth.

Remember

Check that your reading makes sense. If something does not make sense, then stop, go back and read it again.

Understanding word meanings

You will meet lots of new words when you are reading. Make sure you know what these words mean. Be a 'word detective'. Look for clues to help you work out the meaning of words you read.

Clue 1: Read the sentence

Read the rest of the **sentence**. Think of another word that would fit and make sense in the sentence. This is a good clue to the word's meaning.

A big dog came bounding down the path. ⟵ try 'leaping', 'running' or 'jumping'

Clue 2: Think about the subject

Think about what you already know about the subject of the sentence. Read this sentence and think about what the stems of flowers are like:

The flowers swayed on their slender stems. ⟵ this means 'slim' or 'thin'

Clue 3: Think about words you know

The new word might look and sound like a word you know already. The meaning might be linked too. Try it and see if it makes sense.

It was the most wondrous cloak he had ever seen. ⟵ this meaning is like 'wonderful'

Clue 4: Look for word parts

Look at how the word is built up. You might see a word you know and then see a **suffix** on the end.

The soup was watery. ⟵ this means 'like water' (water + y)

The –y suffix is added to lots of words to create **adjectives**, such as fussy and sulky.

Find help from the writer

Sometimes new words are explained for you. You might find a **glossary** in a **non-fiction** book. It gives the meaning of words to do with that subject.

Test yourself

Read these sentences. Write the meaning of the words in blue.
1. She was scared she would tear the delicate lace.
2. Slowly a shape emerged from the shadows.

Remember

Work out the meaning of words when you read them.

Prefixes and suffixes

Prefixes and **suffixes** are added on to words. A prefix is added to the start of a word. A suffix is added to the end of a word.

It is important to know how prefixes and suffixes change words.

The prefix un–

The prefix un– is added to the start of some words. It means 'not'.

he was lucky   he was unlucky   ⟵ he was not lucky

she tied the rope   she untied the rope   ⟵ it was not tied

The suffixes –ful and –less

The suffixes –ful and –less are added to the end of some words to make adjectives. These two suffixes have very different meanings.

lots of **pain** ⟵ **pain**ful   **pain**less ⟶ no **pain**

full of **fear** ⟵ **fear**ful   **fear**less ⟶ no **fear**

The suffixes –er and –est

The suffixes –er and –est are added to adjectives to help compare things.

small ⟶ smaller ⟶ smallest

Goldilocks sat on the smallest chair.   ⟵ the most small

The suffix –ly

The suffix –ly makes words into **adverbs** that tell you how something is done.

He spoke sadly.   ⟵ in a sad way

The suffixes –er, –ness, –ment

These suffixes are added to some words to make **nouns**.

leader   sadness   amazement

Test yourself

1. Think of three new words with the prefix un–, and write them down.

Add a suffix to complete these sentences.

2. The magic was very power____.
3. Thank you for your kind____.
4. My brother is old____ than me.

Remember

Prefixes go on the start of words. Suffixes go on the end of words.

Following a story

When you read a piece of **fiction**, such as a story, always try to follow the **events**, or what is happening.

Off went Jack, followed by the monster.

Here are some ideas to help you follow the story.

Picture the events

As you read, picture what happens in the story. Picture the **characters**. Picture where and when the story takes place. Picture the events happening – imagine you are watching them like a film.

Remember the main events

Stop reading and see if you can remember the main events in the story. Think about the events in the right order. Try telling someone else what happened.

Predict what might happen

Think about what you have read so far. Use this information to **predict** what might happen next. Then read on to see if you were right.

Test yourself

Think about the story 'The gingerbread man'. Number these sentences to show what order the events happen in. The first one has been done for you.

The gingerbread man comes to a river.

An old lady bakes a gingerbread man. *1*

A fox tricks the gingerbread man.

Everyone chases the gingerbread man.

The gingerbread man runs away.

Remember

When you read a story, picture what happens as you read it. Try to remember the main events in order.

Reading and predicting

Read and enjoy the story below. See if you can predict how the story will end.

Fair shares?

There were once two bears called Oscar and Bruno. They were brothers but were very different.

One spring morning the two bears went fishing. Oscar liked fish, but he did not like fishing. He was lazy. He wanted his brother to do the hard work.

But brother Bruno was clever. He knew a way to trick Oscar into working.

'Let us share the work,' Bruno said. 'I'll do the fishing. You can get tired for me.'

Get tired! Oscar did not like that idea very much.

'No way!' Oscar said. 'I'll do the fishing. You can get tired for me.'

'As you wish,' Bruno smiled.

All day, Oscar dived around in the rushing water trying to catch fish. All day, Bruno sat under a tree in the spring sunshine. As he sat, he huffed and puffed, and he puffed and huffed.

'What hard work,' Bruno said in a weary voice. 'I am so tired!'

By the end of the day, Oscar had caught three fish.

'It is hard to share three fish,' Bruno said. 'You take them. I'll have the fish we catch tomorrow. We might get four or five tomorrow …'

Four or five fish! Oscar liked the thought of that. He would let his brother Bruno take the three fish caught today. He would have tomorrow's catch.

So off went Bruno with the three fish. While Oscar had none.

Test yourself

Think about what you have read. Do you think Oscar got his four or five fish the next day? Why, or why not? When you have answered the question, turn to page 63 to see how the story ends.

Understanding the story

It is a good idea to think about a story you have just read. This will help you understand it better.

At school, you might discuss the **characters**, **setting** or **events**. You might ask or answer **questions** about what happened. The questions might begin with some of these words:

When…?   What…?   Where…?   Who…?

Asking and answering questions will help you think more about the events in the story.

Ask questions

Here are some questions about the events in 'Fair shares?'.

1. When did the two bears go fishing?

2. What did Oscar do all day?

3. Where did Bruno sit all day?

4. Who had no fish at the end of the day?

You should go back and look for details in the story to help answer questions like these.

Look for details

This is how you do it.

- Think about what the question is asking.
- Decide which part of the story the question is asking about.
- Go back and find that part of the story.
- Read that part again to find the words that give the answer.

Test yourself

Answer the questions on this page about the story 'Fair shares?' For each question go back and find the part that gives the answer.

Remember

Go back and find the details in the story.

Explaining why

Some questions begin with the word 'Why'. 'Why' questions need you to think about why things happen in stories or why characters do what they do.

Here are two things to remember about 'why' questions.

'Why' questions need a reason

'Why' questions need you to explain or give reasons for what happens in the story. Find the reason in the story. Then start your answer with the word 'because', like this:

Why did Oscar not like fishing?

Because he was lazy and fishing is hard work.

Find clues in the story

Sometimes you need to think very carefully to answer a 'why' question. The reason is not always there in front of you. You must read carefully and look for clues in the story.

You still need to find the right part of the story but you might also need to think about what happened before or what happens after, as a result.

Think about what the story tells you and what you know. Work out the reasons from the clues.

Test yourself

Answer these questions about the story 'Fair shares?' Think carefully about the events and the characters' actions. Make sure you have read the end of the story on page 63.

1. Why did Bruno smile when he said, 'As you wish'?
2. Why did Bruno huff and puff as he sat under the tree?
3. Why did Oscar let Bruno have the three fish?
4. Why was Oscar too tired to go fishing the next day?

Remember

Find the reason in the story or look for clues in what the story tells you.

Thinking about the story

Sometimes you need to think about the whole story, not just one **event**. Here are some examples of things you might think about:

- why an event was important in the story
- why the writer chose the title for the story
- what you think a **character** learnt from the **events**.

These **questions** make you think about what happened in the story. You must use the events to help you explain or give reasons.

Think about the title

The title gives a good clue to what the story is about. It fits with the events. For example, the title of the story on page 9 is 'Fair shares?' This makes you think about what happens in the story. Bruno and Oscar agree to share the work and share the fish – but is it fair? The **question mark** makes you think about that.

Think about an important event

Some events are important because they make the story work. In 'Fair shares?' Bruno tricks his brother into doing all the fishing. Think about how the story would be different if the trick had not worked.

Say what you think

Sometimes questions ask what you think. You must think about the events in the story to give an answer. For example, here is a question about 'Fair shares?'

> Do you think Oscar will be pleased with his brother? Why, or why not?

You need to think about what Bruno did and what happened in the story, to decide on your answer. Then use the events in the story to help explain your answer.

No, Oscar will not be pleased. Not when he realises that he has done all the work but got no fish!

Test yourself

Think about the story on page 9. Answer these questions.

1. Do you think 'Clever Oscar' would be a good title for the story? Give a reason.
2. Do you think what Bruno did to his brother was fair? Explain your answer.

Remember

Use things that happen in the story to explain your ideas about it.

Thinking about characters

Stories are about characters and the things that happen to them. A story tells you a lot about who the characters are, what they look like and what sort of people they are. Look for details and clues to help you understand them better.

Here are some things for you to look for in a story.

Character details

When you read a story, look for words that tell you about a character.

> Otto the fruit seller was tired but happy.

What they say and do

Look out for what characters say and do. These words and actions can show what sort of person the character is.

> 'Let me help you with that,' said Otto, picking up the old man's heavy load.

Words that show

Look for words that show how a character feels or what he or she is thinking.

> Otto frowned as he stood beneath the tree looking up into the branches. Now he had hurt his back, he could no longer reach up to get the best fruit.

Character clues

Look for clues that help you work out what a character is thinking or feeling. Think about the events and what has happened to the character. Imagine what is going on in his or her head – can you read the character's mind?

Test yourself

1. What was Otto's job?
2. What sort of person was Otto? How can you tell?
3. Why is Otto worried when he has a bad back?

Remember

Look for words and details that tell you about the characters. Look for clues in what they say and do.

Reading poems

Poems are special. They have a special shape and a special sound. They look different and sound different from other sorts of writing.

Look at the shape

Look at the shape of the poem and how it is set out on the page.

- Is it split into verses?
- How long are the lines?
- Are words or lines used more than once?
- Is there a pattern?

Read the poem aloud

Read the poem aloud so you can hear how it sounds. Listen for special sound patterns. Think about what the poem is about and how it makes you feel.

When you have read the poem a few times, you could try to learn it off by heart.

Understand the poem

Each time you read the poem, you will notice more details. You will start to understand the poem better. Think about what each line or each verse tells you. Think about what the whole poem is telling you.

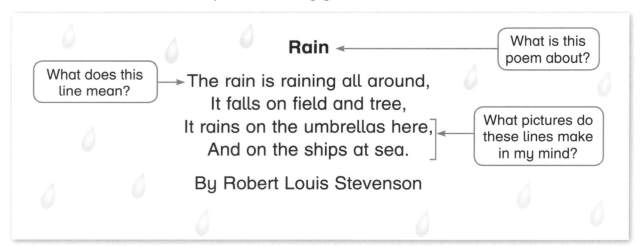

Rain ← What is this poem about?

What does this line mean? → The rain is raining all around,
It falls on field and tree,
It rains on the umbrellas here, ← What pictures do these lines make in my mind?
And on the ships at sea.

By Robert Louis Stevenson

Test yourself

Read the poem 'Rain'. Answer these questions about it.

1. What is the main idea in this poem?
2. The poem says that the rain falls on four things. What are they?
3. Which line tells you that the poet is not on a ship?

Remember

Read the poem a few times and think about what each line or verse tells you.

The poet's words

A **poet** chooses words very carefully. Each word is important to the meaning or the sound of the poem. When you read a poem, think about the words in it and what they say to you.

Word pictures

Poets use words to paint pictures and describe things. When you read a poem, look for the words that help to make a picture in your mind.

> On a soggy day like this,
> Raindrops explode on the window pane.

Think about what the word 'explode' tells you about the raindrops. What do you picture?

Sound patterns

Poets make sounds with words. When you read a poem aloud, listen for the special sound patterns made by the words.

- Listen for words that **rhyme**. They have the same sound at the end.

    Summer sun

    Let's have fun

- Listen for words that begin with the same letter sound.

    In the sizzling summer sun

- Listen for **rhythm** or beat in the poem. Clap along!

    Sun, sun, sun – let's have fun

Slow, slow,
Said the snail,
Slowly laying
His slippery trail.

Busy, busy,
Said the bee,
Buzzing by
Buzzzzzzzzzily.

Test yourself

Look at the poem about the snail and the bee.

1. In the first verse, copy the two rhyming words.
2. What does the word 'slippery' tell you about the snail's trail?
3. In the second verse, write three words that begin with the same letter sound.
4. Why do you think the poet chose the last word?

Remember

Words can paint pictures or make sound patterns – or both!

Reading non-fiction texts

A **non-fiction** text gives you information or **facts** about something. There are lots of different types of non-fiction texts. Here are some examples.

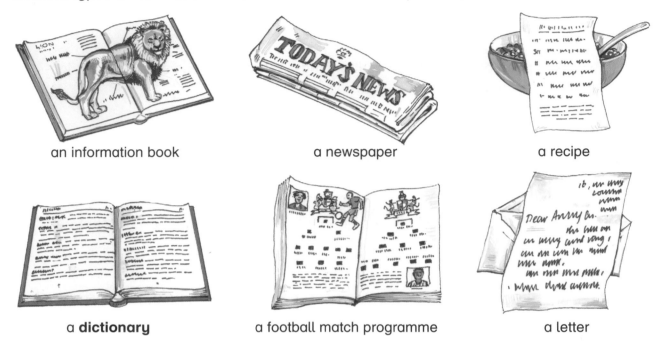

an information book   a newspaper   a recipe

a **dictionary**   a football match programme   a letter

Different types of non-fiction text are ordered in different ways. Some are in **alphabetical order**, some are in date or number order. Some non-fiction texts are organised into different sections or topics.

How to read non-fiction

You read different types of non-fiction text in different ways. You read some non-fiction texts from the start to the end. But sometimes you just choose the bits you want to read.

Before you begin reading:

- look at the title – it will tell you what the text is about
- skim or look quickly through the text to see what sort of text it is and how it is organised
- decide what you want to know or find out – do you need to read all the text or just part of it?

Test yourself

Answer these questions about the non-fiction texts at the top of this page.

1. Which one will be in alphabetical order?
2. Which one might have the title 'How to make perfect cupcakes'?
3. What might you find on a different page of the information book?

Remember

Look through the text to see what type of text you are reading and how it is organised.

Features of information books

An information book gives you information about a topic. The book is organised and set out to help you find the information you want.

Contents and indexes

Non-fiction books often have a **contents** page at the front and an **index** at the back. These help you find the information you need.

Contents	
Dogs	2
Cats	4
Rabbits	6
Mice	8
Fish	10
Snakes	11
Birds	12

Index		
birds 12, 13		hutch 6
cage 12		lead 3
cats 4, 5		mice 8, 9
dogs 2, 3		rabbits 6, 7
exercise 3		snakes 11
fish 10		tank 10

The contents page shows you what is inside the book. It tells you what is on each page.

The index gives a list of subjects and their page numbers. It is in alphabetical order.

What is on a page

Each page in a non-fiction text is set out to help you read the information.

- The **heading** at the top of a page tells you what the page is about.
- **Sub-headings** tell you what each section is about.
- Numbers might tell you what order to read things in.
- Text boxes might make some things stand out.

Test yourself

Answer these questions about the contents and index pages above.

1. What is the book about?
2. How is the information organised in this book?
3. Why are the words in the index in alphabetical order?
4. What would be the heading on page 6?

Remember

The contents page, headings and sub-headings show you how the information is organised.

Finding information

You might read a **non-fiction** text to find information or the answer to a **question**. You can **scan** the text to help you find this information quickly.

Imagine that you are learning about insects and you want to answer this question.

What do caterpillars eat?

You have some information about caterpillars to help you.

Caterpillars are the young of butterflies. They hatch out of eggs.

Caterpillars feed on leaves and other parts of plants. They eat a lot so that they grow bigger. When they are fully grown they spin a cocoon.

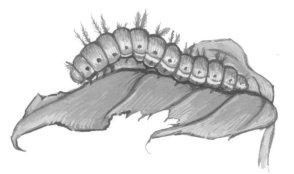

Now you need to find the answer to the question.

How to find the answer quickly

1. Think about the key words in the question.

   What do caterpillars eat?

2. Scan the text to find those words or words that mean the same.

   Caterpillars feed on **leaves and other parts of plants.**

You might not find exactly the same words, but 'feed on' means the same as 'eat'.

3. Read the whole **sentence** to find the answer.

   Caterpillars feed on leaves and other parts of plants.

Sometimes you need more than one piece of information. Scan for the key words again. Or read the sentence before or after.

Test yourself

Use the information on this page about caterpillars to find the answers to these questions.

1. What are caterpillars?
2. Why do caterpillars eat a lot?
3. When do caterpillars spin a cocoon?

Remember

Scan for key words to help you find information about a subject or the answer to a question.

Information from pictures

It is not only words that give information – pictures give information too. A non-fiction book might have photographs, drawings, diagrams or charts.

Photographs and drawings

Pictures can show you what something looks like and help you to understand the information. Always read the **caption** that goes with a picture. The caption tells you what the picture shows. It can also give you extra details.

Butterflies feed on nectar from flowers.

Diagrams and labels

A diagram shows something in detail. Always read the labels on a diagram. The labels point out important details.

long 'tongue' for sucking up nectar

wings covered with tiny scales, which look like dust

Charts and tables

Some information may be set out in a chart or table. This helps you to pick out key **facts** quickly.

	Butterfly	Dragonfly	Ladybird
Wing span in centimetres (cm)	4–6cm across	7–10cm across	1cm across

Test yourself

Use the information on this page to answer these questions.

1. Write three facts about a butterfly's wings.
2. What do butterflies feed on?
3. How does a butterfly suck up food?
4. Which is bigger, a butterfly or a dragonfly?

Remember

Captions and labels on pictures and diagrams give important details and help you understand information.

Reading for information

Read this information carefully. Think about it as you read. Check that it makes sense.

The great recycle

Every week we fill our bins with rubbish. We put our bins out and the rubbish is taken away.

Some of the rubbish is dumped in huge holes in the ground. It rots and gives off smelly gases. Some of the rubbish is burned. It makes smoke that fills the air. This is all very bad for the environment.

Even worse, we are throwing away useful materials. Think about all the paper you use every day. If you throw that away, we have to cut down more trees to make more paper.

Reduce, reuse, recycle!

We all need to reduce or cut down the amount of rubbish we throw away.

Most homes now have special bins for things that can be recycled instead of throwing them away. Glass, paper, metal and some plastics can be recycled and made into new items. Many supermarkets and car parks also have recycling points for clothing, shoes and batteries. This is a good start.

But we could all do more! Some things do not need to be recycled. They can be reused. Don't throw away plastic carrier bags – use them again. Don't throw away those empty jars or pots – use them to store your odds and ends! Don't throw away clothes – give them to a charity shop.

Food waste is another big problem. If you have a compost bin in your garden, you can put things like vegetable peelings in the compost bin rather than in your rubbish bin. Reuse your waste to help feed the plants.

Remember the three Rs – Reduce, Reuse, Recycle and make a difference!

Glossary

environment	the land, sea and air around us
reduce	to cut down (and use less)
recycled	made into something new
reused	used again

Test yourself

Write down three important ideas from what you have read.

Explaining information

Reading **non-fiction** is not just about finding information. Sometimes you need to discuss or explain the ideas to other people. So it is important to think carefully about what you read.

For example, think about the information you read on page 20. Could you explain the information to others?

Explaining ideas

There are lots of **questions** you could be asked about the information on page 20. When you answer questions like this, you need to explain and give reasons. You must use what you read to help you do this.

So think about what you have read. Go back and read parts of the text again. Find the information that will help you explain or give reasons.

- Think about the main ideas.
- Think about what you have learnt from the text.
- Think about why it is important.

Work things out

The text does not always give you an obvious answer. Sometimes you need to use the information you have read to work things out. For example:

> Is it better to reuse a jam jar or recycle it? Why?

The information on page 20 does not tell you the answers but it gives you clues to help work it out.

Think about what it tells us about recycling and reusing. Then decide on your answers, giving a reason for each one.

Test yourself

Read 'The great recycle' again. Then answer these questions.
1. Why is it important to recycle and reuse?
2. Why are more people now recycling? Give two reasons.
3. Explain how a compost bin can help to reduce rubbish.
4. Explain how you could reduce the rubbish in your bin at home.

Remember

Think about what the text tells you to help you explain or give reasons.

Writing in sentences

When we write we usually put our ideas into **sentences**. Each sentence tells the reader one of our ideas.

A sentence must:

- make sense on its own
- give one complete idea
- have a **capital letter** at the start and a **full stop** at the end.

You can write more sentences to add more ideas. For example:

Apples are crispy. They are good for you. I eat an apple every day.

These sentences are **statements**. Each sentence tells the reader something about apples.

How to write a sentence

1. Say the whole sentence in your head before you write it down.
2. Put a capital letter at the start of the first word.
3. Say the sentence in your head word by word as you write it.
4. Put a full stop after the last word.
5. Read the sentence back to check that it makes sense.

Write a command

A **command** is a special type of sentence. It tells the reader to do something – or not to. For example:

Eat an apple every day. Don't eat the pips!

Test yourself

1. Write a sentence about a game you like to play.
2. Write a sentence with the word 'ball' in it.
3. Complete this command: 'Put the cards _____'

Remember

When you write, think in sentences. Say each sentence in your head before you write it down.

Joining ideas together

You can put two ideas or two pieces of information into one sentence. You just need to use one of these special **joining words**:

and   but   or

These words let you carry on a sentence. After the joining word you can add another idea or another piece of information.

idea 1	joining word	idea 2
The queen stood up	and	everyone cheered.
We set off early	but	the bus was late.
It might rain	or	it might be sunny.

How to use joining words

1. Say the whole sentence in your head before you write it.
2. Write the first idea but don't put a full stop at the end.
3. Instead, write the joining word.
4. Then write the second idea.
5. Put a full stop at the end.

Join your writing

If you have a lot of ideas, it is good to use some joining words.

Apples are crispy and have smooth skins. The skins can be red or green. Apple skins are tasty but they can be hard to chew.

Test yourself

A joining word has been used in each of these sentences. Complete the sentences with your own ideas.

1. You can wait here or…
2. Jack ran away but…
3. The phone rang and…

Remember

Use the words 'and', 'but' and 'or' to join two ideas in one sentence.

More joining words

Here are some more **joining words**:

because   when   if   that

These words can help you to write longer **sentences**. They let you say more about your main idea.

Use 'because'

You can use the word 'because' to give a reason or explain an idea. Look at how this sentence carries on after 'because'.

It is important to do some exercise every day because it keeps you fit and healthy.

Use 'when'

You can use the word 'when' to say more about when something happened.

   We went out to play when it stopped raining.

Use 'if'

You can use the word 'if' to show that something might happen if something else does.

   We will be on time if we're quick.

Use 'that'

You can use the word 'that' to add more information.

   I told the teacher that my coat was missing.

Test yourself

Complete these sentences.
1. A dictionary is very useful because...
2. We went to bed when...
3. The snowman will melt if...
4. He sat on the chair that...

Remember

Use the right joining word to add more information into a sentence.

Adding to sentences

You can add extra information into a sentence to say where, when, how or why. Try this when you say a sentence in your head. Start with a simple sentence like this:

Joe went for a walk.

Then add more detail to the sentence. You could tell the reader when Joe went. You might add this to the start of the sentence.

After breakfast, Joe went for a walk.

Or you could use an **adverb** to tell the reader how he went. You might add this into the middle of the sentence.

Joe quickly went for a walk.

Or you could tell the reader where he went. You might add this detail to the end of the sentence.

Joe went for a walk in the park.

Or you could use a joining word and tell the reader why he went:

Joe went for a walk because he wanted some fresh air.

You could even give the reader all this extra information in one sentence!

After breakfast, Joe quickly went for a walk in the park because he wanted some fresh air.

Test yourself

Add some more information to these sentences.
1. Dan rode his bike.   (When? Where?)
2. Carrie slipped out of the door.   (When? How?)
3. The dog ran.   (Where? How?)

Remember

Add some extra details into a sentence to say where, when, how or why things happened.

Using describing words

You can make **sentences** more lively and more interesting by adding words that describe or give extra detail.

Nouns and adjectives

Nouns are words that name people, places or things. Here is a sentence with two nouns.

A man lived in a cottage.

An **adjective** is a word that tells you more about a noun. In this sentence you can add adjectives to describe the man and the cottage.

A jolly old man lived in a tiny, run-down cottage.

When you add words to a noun, you make a **noun phrase**.

man ⟶ jolly old man

The noun phrase has more detail and helps give a better picture of the noun.

Verbs and adverbs

A **verb** describes the action in a sentence. Here is a sentence with a verb.

The goggle-eyed alien ran after the shaggy dog.

The word 'ran' is a verb. You can make the sentence even more interesting by adding an **adverb** to say how he ran.

The goggle-eyed alien ran clumsily after the shaggy dog.

The word 'clumsily' is an adverb. Adverbs tell you more about actions or how **events** happen. They add more detail and help give a better picture of events.

Test yourself

Add adjectives to the nouns to make noun phrases that describe in more detail.

1. The lady was wearing a hat.
2. The wolf climbed the tree.
3. Waves crashed on to the rocks.

Remember

Use adjectives to describe or add detail to nouns. Use adverbs to describe or add detail to verbs.

Past and present tense

You can write sentences in different **tenses**: the present tense or the past tense. Present tense means it is happening now. Past tense means it has already happened.

present tense	past tense
I play cricket. ⟶	I played cricket.
He helps me a lot. ⟶	He helped me a lot.

The past tense of these verbs ends with –ed. Most verbs have this –ed ending.

Verbs that change

Some verbs have a different word for the past tense. For example:

present tense	past tense
He sits down. ⟶	He sat down.
I see three ships. ⟶	I saw three ships.
I go to school. ⟶	I went to school.

If you say these verbs with –ed, it sounds wrong.

I ~~goed~~ to school.

Verbs with –ing

Sometimes –ing is added to the end of verbs, to show that an action is (or was) carrying on. You can use –ing verbs in either the present tense or the past tense but you need an extra verb to complete the sentence.

present tense	past tense
He **is** running. ⟶	He **was** running.
She **is** falling. ⟶	She **was** falling.
I **am** shouting. ⟶	I **was** shouting.
We **are** waiting. ⟶	We **were** waiting.

You must choose the correct word to complete the sentence. The verb changes if there is more than one person.

Test yourself

Complete the present tense and past tense of the verbs in these sentences.

1. The dog bark__.   2. He _____ waiting.

Remember

Choose the right verb or verb ending to show past or present tense.

Capital letters and full stops

Punctuation marks are like signals to the reader.

Capital letters and **full stops** are the signals at the start and end of **sentences**. Every sentence you write needs a capital letter at the start and a full stop at the end.

A capital letter at the start of a sentence says 'GO!'

> **W**e went into the playground.

A full stop at the end of a sentence tells your reader, 'STOP!'

> We went into the playground.

Sentence punctuation

Always try to add capital letters and full stops as you write. Say the sentence, put the capital letter, write the sentence and add the full stop.

If you forget the capital letters and full stops, your reader will not know where to start and stop.

We went into the playground on the grass there was a climbing frame with a rope ladder next to it was a sand pit

Check your punctuation

Proofread your writing when you have finished. Read it aloud in your head. Listen for where each sentence starts and ends. Check that full stops and capital letters are in the right place.

Test yourself

Copy out the lines about the playground, adding the missing capital letters and full stops. One capital letter is there already.

Remember

Every sentence needs a capital letter at the start to say 'GO!' and a full stop at the end to say 'STOP!'

Question marks and exclamation marks

Sometimes a sentence needs a **question mark** or **exclamation mark** rather than a full stop. Question marks and exclamation marks say to the reader: 'Look! This is a special sort of sentence.'

A question mark says:
- this sentence is a **question**
- it is asking something and it needs an answer
- read it with a question in your voice.

An exclamation mark says:
- this sentence is an **exclamation**
- it says something surprising
- read it with feeling.

Writing questions

Questions often begin with question words such as 'What?', 'When?', 'Who?', 'Why?', 'Where?' or 'How?' Sometimes questions begin like this:

Can you do this?   Is this right?

If a sentence asks a question, you always need to put a question mark at the end.

Writing exclamations

If you write an exclamation, always put an exclamation mark at the end. Exclamations are often short. Some exclamations are just one word.

What a surprise!   Wow!   How scary!   Great!

Test yourself

Add the punctuation mark needed to complete each sentence.
1. That is amazing
2. What time is it
3. Can I help you
4. Help

Remember

Questions need a question mark to show that they are asking something. Exclamations need an exclamation mark to show that something is surprising.

More capital letters

Capital letters are special letters. We only use them at the start of special words. The first word in a **sentence** starts with a capital letter. So do the lines of a poem and the first word of a title or **heading**.

Special nouns

Some special **nouns**, like those shown below, need a capital letter at the start.

- names of people

  Jack, Sihab, Emma

- names of places

  Uganda, Devon, Leeds

- days of the week

  Thursday, Saturday

- months of the year

  February, August

- the word 'I'

  _I_

How to write capital letters

Make sure you form capital letters correctly and that they are the right way round. Notice that:

- many capital letters are a different shape from their **lower case letters**.

  a A   b B   d D   e E

- some capital letters are the same shape as their lower case letters but taller.

  c C   o O   s S   v V

Make sure that all your capital letters are the right size. They should be the same size as the tall letters, such as b, d, f, h, k. (For more information on handwriting, see page 62.)

Don't mix up capital letters and lower case letters – and don't put capital letters in the middle of words!

woRds ✗

Test yourself

Copy the sentence below. Add capital letters where they are needed.

  on sunday i went to see my friends ben and jacob.

Remember

Use capital letters at the start of names and for the word 'I'.

Commas and inverted commas

Commas

A **comma** looks like a **full stop** with a tail. Commas are used to show breaks in a sentence.

You might write a sentence with a list in it. You put a comma after each item in the list to show the breaks between them.

In the bag there was a bus ticket, a purse, two old photos and a letter.

You do not need a comma between the last two items in a list. Use the word 'and' instead.

Inverted commas

How will I ever get home?

Inverted commas (or speech marks) are used to show when a **character** in a story is saying something.

With speech bubbles, what the person says goes inside the speech bubble.

In the same way, with inverted commas, what the person says goes inside the inverted commas.

'How will I ever get home?' cried the girl.

The words at the end are added on to show who is speaking.

Test yourself

Copy these sentences and add the commas.
1. I had pizza salad and ice cream for tea.
2. In my team were Alice Molly Freddie and Dan.
3. Copy this sentence and underline what the person says.
   'Stop!' shouted the man.

Remember

Commas go between items in a list. Inverted commas go round words that are spoken.

Apostrophes

An **apostrophe** looks like a **comma** but it floats in the air between letters. There are two types of apostrophe.

Missing letters

Sometimes words are written using short forms, rather than writing them out in full.

did not → didn't ← the letter o is missing

I am → I'm ← the letter a is missing

The short forms have an apostrophe to show that there is a missing letter.
The apostrophe goes in the space where the missing letter would be.

I have → Ive → I've ← The apostrophe goes where the letters ha would be.

Make sure you put the apostrophe in the right place. Think where the missing letter or letters would be.

Belonging

Use –'s (say 'apostrophe s') to show that something belongs to someone.

Meg's house

Ravi's coat

the man's dog

Test yourself

1. Write the short form of these words using apostrophes.
   cannot   it is   I will
2. Write this sentence correctly.
   I didnt hear Marks name.

Remember

In short forms, think about where the missing letter(s) would be. Put the apostrophe in their space.

Segmenting words

You can spell lots of short words by **segmenting** them into sounds or **phonemes** first.

Here is a

Break this word down into phonemes and then count them.

There are four phonemes in this word. __ __ __ __

Now say each phoneme in turn and write the letters that make the sounds.

f-r-o-g

Two letters, one sound

Sometimes two letters make one sound.

This is a

This word has four sounds or phonemes, but five letters.
Two letters, c and h, make one sound, 'ch'.

b-e-n-ch

Two-letter endings

In short words, the sounds 'f', 'l', 's', 'z' and 'k' are spelt with two letters if they come after a short **vowel**.

off   tell   fuss   fizz   back

At the end of a word, the 'v' sound is nearly always spelt –ve.

have   give   love

Test yourself

Write the name of each picture.

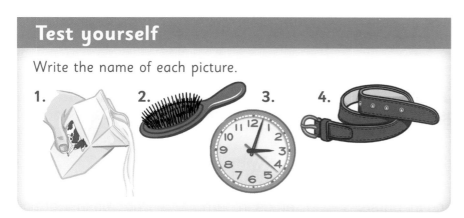

1.   2.   3.   4.

Remember

You can spell lots of short words by segmenting them into phonemes and writing down the letters.

Spelling long vowel sounds

Lots of words have long **vowel** sounds. Most long vowel sounds need two or more letters to write them.

s-p-oo-n   l-ea-f   ch-air

Spelling words with long vowel sounds can be tricky because there is more than one way to spell most of these sounds. Make sure you know the different ways to spell the long vowel sounds on these pages.

Long vowel sounds

Long 'ee' sound

'ee' as in 'bee'   'ea' as in 'ice cream'   'e-e' as in 'these'   'ie' as in 'thief'

Long 'a' sound

'ai' as in 'snail'   'ay' as in 'tray'   'a-e' as in 'plate'

Long 'i' sound

'ie' as in 'pie'   'i-e' as in 'kite'   'igh' as in 'light'   'y' as in 'fly'

Long 'o' sound

'oa' as in 'boat'   'ow' as in 'snow'   'o-e' as in 'bone'   'oe' as in 'toe'

Long 'oo' sound

'oo' as in 'spoon'   'ue' as in 'glue'   'u-e' as in 'cube'   'ew' as in 'stew'

Long 'or' sound

'or' as in 'fork'   'au' as in 'dinosaur'   'aw' as in 'paw'   'ore' as in 'score'

Long 'ur' sound

'ir' as in 'bird'   'ur' as in 'burst'   'er' as in 'fern'   'ear' as in 'Earth'

Long 'air' sound

'air' as in 'chair'

'ear' as in 'bear'

'are' as in 'square'

Long 'ear' sound

'ear' as in 'tear'

'eer' as in 'deer'

'ere' as in 'sphere'

Long 'oy' sound

'oy' as in 'toy'

'oi' as in 'coin'

Long 'ar' sound

'ar' as in 'car'

Long 'ow' sound

'ow' as in 'cow'

'ou' as in 'spout'

Unstressed 'er' sound

'er' as in 'dinner'

Which spelling?

When you spell a word with a long vowel sound, you need to choose the correct spelling for the word. For example, which is the correct spelling for the long vowel sound in this word?

It could be any of these…

o-e   oa   ow   oe

…but the correct spelling is 'coat', with 'oa' for the long vowel sound.

Test yourself

Write the names of these pictures. Choose the correct spellings for the long vowel sounds.

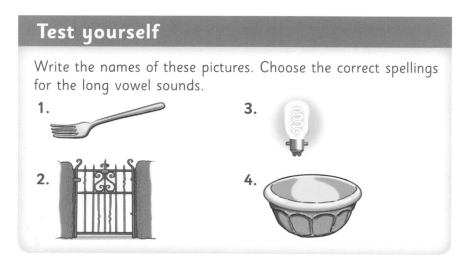

1.

3.

2.

4.

Remember

Long vowel sounds can be tricky to spell. Choose the correct spelling for the word.

Spelling longer words

Some words are too long to break into **phonemes**. First you need to break them into smaller words.

Compound words

Compound words are made from two smaller words joined together.

> **today** = to + day   **football** = foot + ball

You can spell compound words by saying the two words and spelling each one in turn.

Say the syllables

It is easier to spell longer words if you break them into **syllables**. Syllables are the beats in the word. You can hear the syllables when you say the word.

important	→	im-por-tant (three syllables)
remembering	→	re-mem-ber-ing (four syllables)
hippopotamus	→	hip-po-po-ta-mus (five syllables)

Say and write each syllable in turn.

Words and suffixes

Some long words are made up of a short word and a **suffix**. You can spell these words by writing the short word and then adding the suffix.

enjoy-ment	play-ful	mad-ness	care-less	bad-ly
pave-ment	hope-ful	sad-ness	hope-less	quick-ly

Test yourself

Say the names of these pictures. Listen for the syllables or smaller words. Then write down the words.

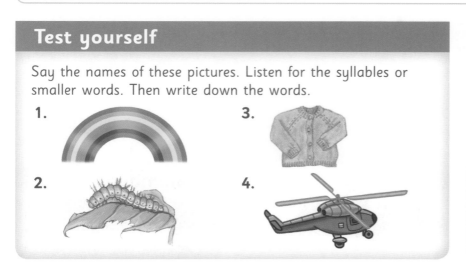

1.

2.

3.

4.

Remember

Break a long word up into smaller parts. Write the word one part at a time.

Word endings

Word endings can be tricky to spell. When you say the word, the sounds at the end are not always clear. Some endings are found on lots of words so it is important to learn to spell them.

The −er ending: thunder   summer   better   letter

Ruby Eastwood
17 Pear Grove
Hoppleton
Drovesbury
DR5 8PQ

Different sounds and spellings

Some word endings are not spelt as they sound. You need to learn these endings and how to spell them.

The −le ending

This sounds like 'l' or 'ul' but is spelt −le.

table   little   kettle   apple

The −el, −al, −il endings

These sound like the −le ending but have a different spelling.

pencil   model   travel   tunnel   metal

The −tion ending

This sounds like 'shun' but is spelt −tion.

station   nation   fiction

The −et ending

The last syllable can sound like 'it', but you must remember to spell it −et.

blanket   pocket   market   jacket

Test yourself

Write two more words with each of these word endings. Think of words that are not on this page.

−et   −le   −el   −tion

Remember

Learn to spell word endings that are found on lots of words.

Adding –s and –es

Singular and plural

If there is more than one of something, you add –s or –es on the end of the word. This makes the **singular** word into a **plural**.

When to add –s

With most words you add –s on the end to make them plural.

one star   ⟶   lots of stars

one cat   ⟶   two cats

one sweet   ⟶   three sweets

You can hear the 's' (or 'z') sound at the end when you say the plural word.

When to add –es

With some words you add –es.

one bench   ⟶   two benches

one box   ⟶   three boxes

one wish   ⟶   lots of wishes

The –es ending sounds different. It makes an 'iz' sound, as in 'box-iz'. This 'iz' sound reminds you to add –es on the end instead of –s.

Words ending –y

If a word ends with –y, you change the y to i before you add –es.

one baby   ⟶   two babies

Verb endings

You can use the same rules to add –s or –es to **verbs**.

help   ⟶   helps

rush   ⟶   rushes

try   ⟶   tries

Remember

Use the rules on this page to add –s or –es to nouns and verbs.

Test yourself

Write the names of these pictures.

1.

2.

3.

4.

Adding –ing and –ed

More verb endings

Verbs often end with –ing or –ed. You add –ing to show that something is happening, and –ed to show that something has happened. Write the verb first and then add the ending.

play + ing = playing   jump + ing = jumping
play + ed = played   jump + ed = jumped

Be careful, though! You cannot always hear the –ed clearly. Sometimes it sounds like a 't' on the end, as in 'jumped'.

Verbs ending –e

If a verb ends with –e, you leave off the e when you add –ed or –ing.

hide + ing = hiding   smile + ed = smiled

Verbs ending –y

If a verb ends with a **consonant** and –y, you change the y to i before you add –ed.

cry + ed = cried

Don't do this with –ing or you will get ii. You add –ing.

cry + ing = crying

Double letters

Sometimes, you double the last letter of the verb before you add –ing or –ed. You do this for words with short **vowels**.

hop + ing = hopping   stop + ed = stopped

Adding –er, –est, –y

Use the same rules to add –er, –est and –y to words.

fancy + er = fancier   sad + est = saddest   ice + y = icy

Test yourself

1. Add –ing to these words.
   a throw **b** smile **c** drop **d** come
2. Add –ed to these words.
   a hope **b** ask **c** try **d** clap

Remember

Use these rules to help you add –ing, –ed, –er, –est and –y to words.

Special spellings

Some **phonemes** have special spellings in some words. Look out for words with these spellings and try to remember them.

The 'w' and 'f' sounds

The 'w' sound is spelt **wh** in these words.

| when | wheel | while | where | whisper |

The 'f' sound is spelt **ph** in these words.

| phone | phonics | graph | alphabet | dolphin |

The 'j' and 's' sounds

The 'j' sound is spelt **g** if it comes before e, i or y.

| giant | genie | gym | magic | giraffe | energy |

The 'j' sound is spelt **–ge** at the end of words, or **–dge** after a short **vowel**.

| page | change | huge | | badge | bridge | edge |

The 's' sound is spelt **c** if it comes before e, i or y.

| ice | city | fancy | circle | cement |

The 'k' sound

The 'k' sound is spelt **k** if it comes before e, i or y.

| kettle | skin | sulky | kitten | keep |

The 'k' sound is spelt **c** before other letters.

| camp | coach | curl | cream | clock |

Silent letters kn–, wr–

In some words the 'n' sound is spelt **kn**.

| knock | know | knee | knit |

In some other words the 'r' sound is spelt **wr**.

| write | wrote | wrong | wrap |

Remember

Learn which words have these special spellings for some phonemes.

Test yourself

1. Write the correct spelling of these words.
   - **a** elefant
   - **b** nife
   - **c** charj
   - **d** ritten
   - **e** mise

Using spelling patterns

Sometimes learning to spell one word can help you to spell other words with the same spelling pattern. For example, learn to spell the word 'all' and you can spell all these words too.

| –all | call ball tall fall hall wall stall |

Here are some more groups of words with the same spelling pattern.

–old	old cold gold hold told fold
–atch	catch match patch snatch
–key	key monkey donkey turkey

These spelling patterns are trickier. But if you learn to spell one tricky word, then the other words in the group are easy.

–alk	walk talk chalk stalk
–other	other another mother brother
–ould	could would should
–ind	find kind mind blind behind
–ove	move prove improve remove

These tricky spelling patterns all come after a 'w' sound. Notice how the vowel sound is spelt.

wa–	was wash want watch wander
war–	war warm warn towards forwards
wor–	word work worm world worth

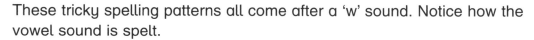

Test yourself

Write a rhyming word that has the same spelling pattern.

1. any and _any
2. most and _ost
3. wild and _ild
4. there and __ere

Remember

You can learn to spell groups of words by looking for the same spelling patterns.

Learning to spell tricky words

As you have learnt, lots of words have tricky bits that are not spelt as they sound.

said your they once was love are do

Look ⟶ say ⟶ cover ⟶ write ⟶ check

You can learn to spell tricky words like this by following these five steps.

1. First **look** at the word.
2. Now **say** the word, saying all the sounds in it. Can you spot the tricky bit? Underline it so you remember it.
3. Then **cover** the word.
4. Now try to **write** it. Think carefully about the tricky bit.
5. Finally, **check** your spelling to see if you are right.

Repeat this set of steps three times for each tricky word you are learning to spell.

---

30 tricky words

anybody	busy	every	half	Mr	school
beautiful	climb	eye	hour	Mrs	sugar
because	clothes	father	house	only	sure
both	eight	friend	laugh	people	water
break	even	great	money	pretty	who

Test yourself

Learn to spell the tricky words in the box. Use the five steps above to help you. (You could also ask an adult to test you – ask the adult to say the words and see if you can write them down.)

Remember

Learn to spell tricky words. Use the five steps: look – say – cover – write – check.

Which word is which?

Some words sound the same but they have different meanings and different spellings. These words are called **homophones**, and they can be confusing.

pair   pear

You need to know which word is which so you can use the right spelling at the right time.

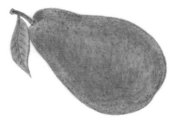

a pair of socks (two of them)   a pear on a tree (a fruit)

Homophone sentences

It helps to learn to spell these words in **sentences**. A sentence can make clear which word is which. Here are some sentences for you to remember.

I see the sea.

I blew up a blue balloon.

I spent the whole day digging a hole.

My teddy bear is old and bare.

I felt weak all last week.

We won three one.

It says ten to two on my watch too.

Some words are not homophones but they are very similar. It can be easy to mix these up too.

It was quite quiet.

Pictures can help

Sometimes a picture can help you remember a spelling.

see

eye

Test yourself

Write the missing word to complete each sentence.

1. I like baked b_____.
2. Come over h_____.
3. I shall w_____ my coat today.

Proofreading your writing

Always **proofread** or check your writing carefully when you finish it. Look for any mistakes in spelling, grammar or **punctuation**.

Check the sentence grammar

Read your writing aloud in your head. Listen for words that do not sound right. Think about the correct word and write it in.

were
We ran down to the beach but they ~~was~~ gone.

sang
He ~~singed~~ a song as he went along.

taller
I am ~~more tall~~ than Steve.

Check the punctuation

As you read your writing, check that all your **sentences** have **capital letters** and **full stops**. Think about the other punctuation marks you know. Look carefully. If you have missed any, add them in.

W
I could go to the park, cinema or library. ~~w~~hat do you think?

don't   *Becky*   *Friday*
I ~~dont~~ think ~~becky~~ can come on ~~friday~~.

Check the spelling

To find spelling mistakes you need to look very carefully. Underline the part of the word that looks wrong. Try to find or remember the correct spelling and write it in.

Everybody   *parents*
~~Evryboddy~~ was there. I saw Jack standing with his ~~pairents~~.

Test yourself

There is a mistake in each sentence. Write the correct word.

1. He hasnt come yet.
2. She am waiting outside.
3. She gived it away.
4. They where late.
5. They ran everywere.

Remember

Read your writing aloud in your head. Check your work carefully when you have finished writing.

Thinking of story ideas

When you write a story, start by thinking about stories you have read. Think about what the stories were about, how they started and what happened. Use these ideas to help you write your own story.

Borrow an idea

You could write a story that follows the same pattern as a story you know. Or you might begin your story like a story you have read.

I'll write a story about a genie in a box.

Choose the story ingredients

When you have an idea for your story, think about the main story ingredients:

- the **characters** – who is the story about?
- the **setting** – where and when does the story take place?
- the **events** – what happens and how?

Tell a good story

Try retelling stories aloud that you have read. Think about how stories sound and what kind of language they use. Keep the sound in your head as you tell it. If you can tell a good story, you will soon learn to write a good story too.

Test yourself

Think of ideas for a story called 'The magic potion'. Think about stories you know. Then write down some ideas for characters, setting and events.

Remember

You can get ideas for characters, settings, events and story language by thinking about stories you have read.

Planning the story

It is a good idea to think through your whole story before you start writing. Think about how your story will begin, what will happen in the middle and how it will end.

You could draw a story map or make a **storyboard** like this to help you think through **events**.

If there are lots of things happening in the middle of your story, add more boxes in the middle of your storyboard.

Make a plan

Think through the events of your story in order. It helps to make a plan. You could also write ideas on a planning frame, such as a **flowchart**.

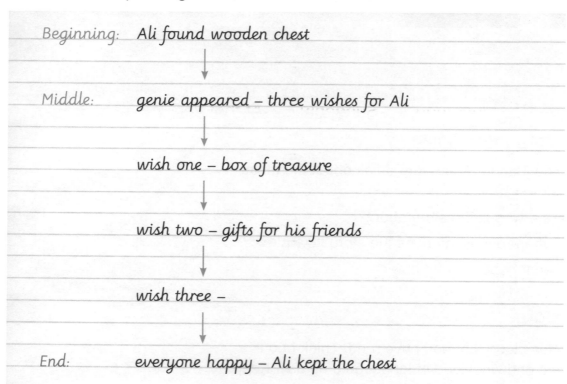

Tell someone your story. Ask them what they think of it.

Using time links

In a story, everything must happen in order. The events should link together. One thing happens. Then something else happens. Then something else, and so on.

But it sounds a bit boring if you keep writing:

Then… Then… Then…

Instead you can use special **linking words** to order and link events.

> Once… Soon… Later… Meanwhile…

Time link words and phrases

Linking words and **phrases** can tell your reader when events happened.

> Early one morning… The next day… Later that night…

Some linking words and phrases show that a long time has passed.

> Eventually… After a long time… Finally… Much later…

Some linking words and phrases show that something happened quickly. You can use these when there is an exciting or surprising event in your story.

> All of a sudden… Just then… Suddenly… At that very moment…

Time links in your story

Try writing linking words or phrases on your story plan. This will remind you to start each new event in your story with a time link.

The next day **the genie appeared again.**

Test yourself

Write the next event after these linking words.

1. Cinderella sat down and began to cry. All of a sudden…
2. Jack climbed and climbed and climbed. Eventually…
3. Hansel and Gretel fell fast asleep in the forest. The next morning…

Remember

Use time link words and phrases to link together the events in your story.

Writing story sentences

Write your story one **sentence** at a time. Think about what you want to write and say the sentence before you write it down. Make your sentence sound like a story sentence.

1. Say the sentence aloud or in your head.
2. Ask yourself, 'Do I like that sentence?'
3. Improve the sentence.
4. Then write it down.

How to improve a sentence

You can improve a sentence by adding something or changing a word.

You might:

- add a word such as an **adverb** or an **adjective** to describe

    purple   *suddenly*
    A puff of ∧ smoke ∧ appeared.

- change a word to a better or more interesting one (try a few words out before you choose one, so you can select the best word rather than the first one that comes into your head).

    The golden coins shone in the sunlight.   ⟨ sparkled... shimmered... glistened... glinted...? ⟩

- use a **joining word** to add more information to your sentence.

    Max fell fast asleep *because* he was so tired.

When you are happy with the sentence, write it down.

Test yourself

Think of a better word to use in place of the blue word in each sentence.

1. The little mouse looked round the corner.
2. The cake was nice.
3. 'Please let me go,' said the tiny alien.

Remember

Say your sentence aloud. Do you like it? Improve it. Write it down.

Adding story detail

As you write your story, try to make it sound interesting, like the stories you read in books. Add details and **description** to interest your reader and bring your story to life. Think like a real story writer. Make your stories sparkle!

How to write good stories

Here are some ideas to help you write better stories.

- Add adjectives to describe the **setting** so your reader can picture the place.

  The woods were dark and overgrown…

- Add details about the **characters**, using adjectives, adverbs and joining words to tell your reader who the characters are, what they look like and how they feel.

  Everyone knew old Mr Anderson and his amazing hats.

  The princess sighed sadly as a tear fell down her face.

- Add details to make the **events** sound funny or exciting – for example, an **exclamation** might make your reader want to keep reading.

  Splash! Something landed in the water right next to her.

- Use some special story language.

  It was a great, big, enormous rabbit…

- Keep the storyteller's **voice** in your head as you write – try out ideas to see how they sound before you write them down.

Test yourself

Make this event sound more interesting by adding details, description or some story language.

  Then Sammy saw something in the sea.

Remember

Think like a storyteller. Use details, words and sentences to make your story sound like a story in a book.

Checking your writing

When you are writing, stop every now and then. Go back to the start and read your story through. Check that it makes sense and sounds right. If something sounds odd, change it. For example, you might be writing about a **character** and then half way through start using the word 'I'.

Josh peeked inside. He gasped. I was amazed.

It is important to correct mistakes like this. Here you could change 'I' to 'Josh' or 'He'.

Check the tense

In stories, you usually write as if **events** have already happened. The past **tense** is used for this.

Josh went and looked in the garden shed.

But sometimes you might forget. You might suddenly start writing in the present tense, as if things are happening right now.

Josh turns the key and carefully opens the lid. Something is gleaming.

Listen for sudden changes from the past to present tense. Change the **verbs** so you keep to the same tense all the way through.

       turned   *opened*   *was*
Josh ~~turns~~ the key and carefully ~~opens~~ the lid. Something ~~is~~ gleaming.

Check that verbs agree

Listen for other verbs that do not sound right. Think about the correct word and write it in.

                          were
All the children ~~was~~ playing outside.

Writing a poem

Think of ideas

Before you start writing, think about the subject. Write down any words and ideas that come into your head. For example, to write a poem about ice cream, think about ice cream! Write down interesting **nouns** and **adjectives**.

> *chocolate chip   vanilla   scoop   juice   creamy*
> *raspberry ripple   rocky road   biscuit   melting   smooth*
> *strawberry   wafer   cornet   chilled   ice-cold*

Choose a poem shape

Think about poems you have read and choose a shape or pattern for your poem. You might decide to:

- group your ideas into verses
- use a sound pattern like **rhythm** or **rhyme**
- use a repeated line or **phrase**.

Write line by line

Look at the words and start to make up lines for your poem. Write your poem one line at a time.

You don't need to write in **sentences**. A line can just be a few words that go well together. But don't forget to give the first word of each line a **capital letter**.

Choose the most interesting words, or words that sound good together. Say each line and improve it before writing it down.

Keep reading your poem aloud to make sure it sounds good.

Ice cream

One raspberry ripple
Two chocolate chips
Three rocky roads
Four strawberry dips.

Five squirts of juice
Six toffee swirls
Seven crispy wafers
Eight biscuit curls.

Nine vanilla cornets
Melt in the sun
Ten happy children
Having ice cream fun!

Test yourself

Read the poem 'Ice cream'. Then write a poem of your own about pizza, sweets, fruit or another sort of food.

Remember

Say each line of your poem before you write it. Keep reading what you have written.

Writing for different purposes

There are lots of different reasons for writing. Sometimes you write to tell people something or to give information. This is called **non-fiction** writing. There are lots of different types of non-fiction writing.

Here are some examples of different writing tasks.

instructions to tell others how to play your favourite game

a postcard to tell your best friend about your holiday

a letter to invite a friend to a special party

a 'wanted' poster to describe a bank robber

a leaflet or booklet to give information about a wildlife garden

Think about what you have read

Always start by thinking about things you have read. If you are writing a letter, think about letters you have read. If you are writing instructions, think about instructions you have used. Try to:

- picture how it was set out on the page
- think about what it told you
- remember how it sounded.

This will help you to make your writing look and sound right.

Test yourself

Look at the writing tasks on this page. For each task, think of something you have read that will help you to do that piece of writing.

Remember

Think about a text you have read, how it was set out, what it said and how it sounded. Use it to help you with your writing.

Planning what to write

Don't just start writing. Your ideas will come out all mixed up. Always stop and think about what you are going to write about before you begin. Write down your ideas or make a plan to help you organise them.

Think about the order

If you are writing about **events** or things that happen in a special order, think through the order. You could write or draw the events on a map or **flowchart** like this one.

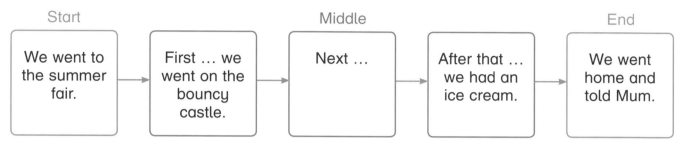

Start
| We went to the summer fair. | → | First … we went on the bouncy castle. | → | Middle Next … | → | After that … we had an ice cream. | → | End We went home and told Mum. |

Organise your ideas

If you are writing information about a topic, think about what you know about it. Write down your ideas. Use a topic web like this to group ideas together. Write the main topic in the middle. Then add your ideas round the outside.

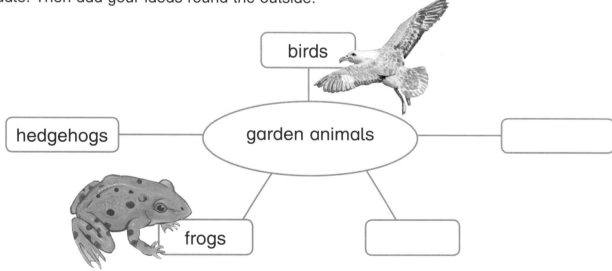

Write down any useful words to do with the topic, and remember to use them in your writing. For example, if you are writing about garden animals:

Useful words: habitat   shelter

Test yourself

1. Add another event to the middle box in the flowchart.
2. Add some more ideas to the 'garden animals' topic web.

Remember

Stop, think and organise before you start writing. Plan what you will write.

Writing ideas in sentences

When you start writing, put your ideas into **sentences**. Write one sentence at a time. Make each sentence add more information about your topic.

Imagine that you are writing about hedgehogs. Start by writing a 'main idea' sentence.

> *Hedgehogs are small animals with spikes or spines.*

Then you will want to tell your reader more about hedgehogs and their spines. Put these ideas into two or three more sentences. You could use a **joining word** in a sentence to help you add more detail or to explain.

> *Hedgehogs are small animals with spikes or spines. The spines help to keep them safe. Hedgehogs roll up into a ball when they are scared or in danger.*

Write descriptions

When you are writing a **description** of something, you still start with a 'main idea' sentence. Then add some more sentences to describe different features.

> *Hedgehogs are small brown animals. They are covered with sharp, prickly spikes or spines. Hedgehogs have pointed faces and small eyes.*

Write about real events

When you are writing about something that happened, start with a 'main idea' sentence that says what you did. Then write more sentences to tell the reader all the details. You will find an example of this on page 57.

Test yourself

Here are two 'main idea' sentences. Write two or three more sentences to follow each main idea.

1. We had a picnic on the beach.
2. An ant is an insect.
3. My favourite flowers are sunflowers.

Remember

Write a 'main idea' sentence and then add more sentences to give the reader interesting details.

Non-fiction words

When you are writing information, it is important to use the right words. Think about what you are writing. Remember to use words linked to the topic. Always choose the best, most exact words.

- If you are explaining how plants grow, think about the **nouns** you use:

  > root   shoot   seedling   compost

- If you are writing a recipe, think about the **verbs** you use:

  > slice   mix   chop   stir   blend

- If you are writing a description of a fruit, think about the **adjectives** you use:

  > juicy   sweet   sticky   ripe   round

- If you are writing instructions, you might also decide to use **adverbs**:

  > carefully   slowly   neatly

Choose the right words

The first words that come into your head might not be the best words. So say the sentence in your head and improve it before you write it down.

'Cut the bread into bits.' ⟶ Slice the bread into thin strips.

Test yourself

One noun in each sentence is in blue. Think of a better noun to use in the sentence.

1. The first bits of snow began to fall.
2. Fill the flowerpot with dirt.
3. Rabbits live in holes underground.

Remember

Non-fiction writing needs exact words. Think about useful words linked to the topic you are writing about.

How does it sound?

When you read something, you can hear the sound of the writer's **voice** in your head. Different types of writing have a different sound. For example, an invitation to a grand **event** sounds very **formal** and polite.

 The Queen of Hearts requests the pleasure of your company.

Different voices

There are many different voices for different types of writing. Here are some more voices to listen out for and copy.

- To write a friendly letter, you might use a chatty voice.

Do you remember when Dad fell in the pool? It was so funny! ← this voice might use **questions** and **exclamations** to sound chatty

- To give instructions, you might use a bossy voice.

Close the lid of the box. ← this voice uses **commands** to tell the reader what to do – start with a bossy **verb**

- To give information, you use a factual voice.

Butterflies are found in many gardens. ← this voice uses **statements** to give clear **facts**

Choose the right voice

You need to choose the right voice for your writing. Think of something you have read and how it sounded. Make your writing sound like that.

1. Say each **sentence** in your head before you write it.
2. Imagine yourself saying the sentence in the writer's voice.
3. Write the sentence and then read it back to check that it sounds right.

Test yourself

1. Write a question in a letter to a friend in hospital.
2. Write a command to help keep the book corner tidy.

Remember

Choose a suitable voice for your writing. Keep reading it to check that it sounds right.

Writing an account

Sometimes you might write an account about **events** or something that happened to you.

Here Umar writes about his day out at a summer fair. Umar drew pictures on a **flowchart** to plan what he would write. Then he wrote about the events in the order they happened.

The labels show what Umar was thinking as he wrote his sentences.

> My first sentence says when, where and what I am writing about.

On Saturday we went to the summer fair at school. I went with my dad and sister. When we got there it was very busy. We were very excited.

> I've got to write about the events in order.

First, we went on the bouncy castle. It was great fun bouncing all over the place. Dad said we looked like mad kangaroos!

> I'll put an **exclamation mark** because this is funny!

> 'Next' is a good **linking word** to what happened next.

Next we went round all the stalls and had a go at all the games. I won a football in the penalty shoot-out game.

After that we were very hot so we had an ice cream. The ice cream was melting fast. My fingers were sticky with strawberry ice cream. My sister had a big messy splodge on her white T-shirt.

> These will give a good picture of how we looked.

When we got home we gave Mum a balloon and told her about the penalty shoot-out. It was a great day.

> This statement is a good way to end.

Test yourself

Write an account of a special day out that you can remember well. Add details to make it more interesting for the reader.

Remember

Plan what you are going to write. Think through the order. Make it interesting for the reader.

Writing a postcard or diary

You can write about special **events** on postcards or in diaries. Postcards and diaries are set out in different ways.

Send a postcard

You might write postcards to tell friends and relatives about what you have been doing on holiday. There is only room for a few **sentences**.

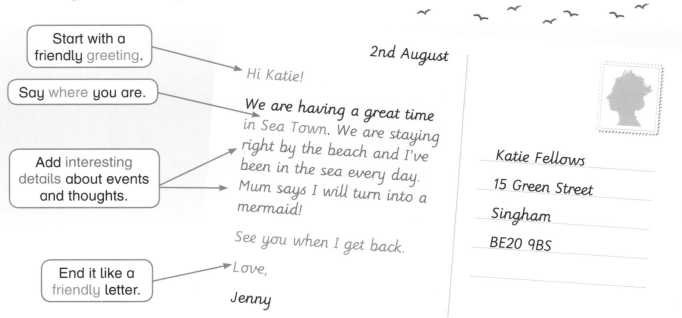

Start with a friendly greeting.

Say where you are.

Add interesting details about events and thoughts.

End it like a friendly letter.

2nd August

Hi Katie!

We are having a great time in Sea Town. We are staying right by the beach and I've been in the sea every day. Mum says I will turn into a mermaid!

See you when I get back.

Love,

Jenny

Katie Fellows

15 Green Street

Singham

BE20 9BS

Keep a diary

You might write a diary to remember events or interesting things you have done each day. Each piece of writing starts with the day or date of the event. You can write about what happened and how you felt. Here is a page from Jenny's holiday diary.

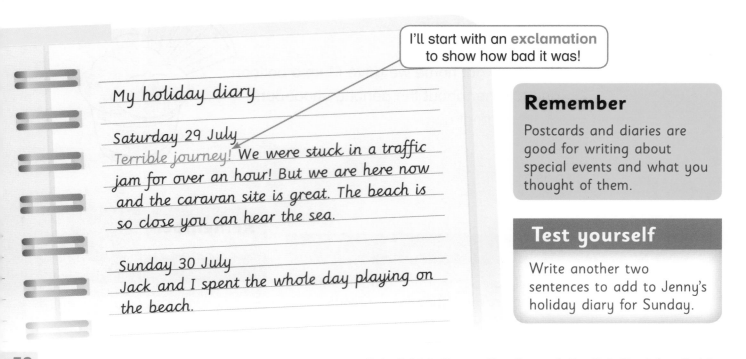

I'll start with an **exclamation** to show how bad it was!

My holiday diary

Saturday 29 July
Terrible journey! We were stuck in a traffic jam for over an hour! But we are here now and the caravan site is great. The beach is so close you can hear the sea.

Sunday 30 July
Jack and I spent the whole day playing on the beach.

Remember

Postcards and diaries are good for writing about special events and what you thought of them.

Test yourself

Write another two sentences to add to Jenny's holiday diary for Sunday.

Writing to give information

You write **reports** or leaflets to give the reader information about something. The information should be well organised. You could use **headings** and **sub-headings** to show what each part is about.

Here is some information that Tarun wrote about animals found in the school wildlife garden. The labels show you what Tarun was thinking as he wrote his report.

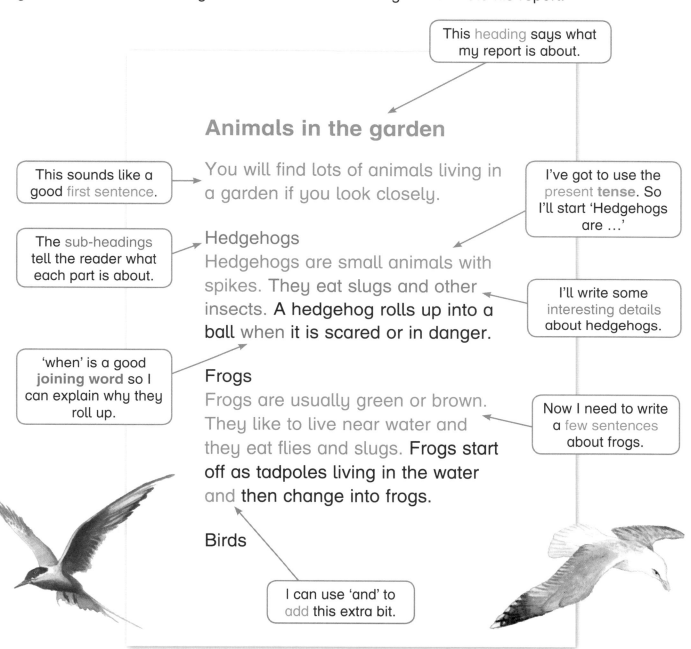

This heading says what my report is about.

Animals in the garden

This sounds like a good first sentence.

You will find lots of animals living in a garden if you look closely.

I've got to use the present **tense**. So I'll start 'Hedgehogs are …'

The sub-headings tell the reader what each part is about.

Hedgehogs
Hedgehogs are small animals with spikes. They eat slugs and other insects. A hedgehog rolls up into a ball when it is scared or in danger.

I'll write some interesting details about hedgehogs.

'when' is a good **joining word** so I can explain why they roll up.

Frogs
Frogs are usually green or brown. They like to live near water and they eat flies and slugs. Frogs start off as tadpoles living in the water and then change into frogs.

Now I need to write a few sentences about frogs.

Birds

I can use 'and' to add this extra bit.

Test yourself

Write three or four sentences to go under the heading 'Birds' in Tarun's report. Try to use some words such as 'and', 'but' or 'when'.

Remember

Organise your ideas to help the reader. Use headings, sub-headings and joining words.

Writing instructions

You write instructions to tell someone how to do something. You might tell the reader how to make something, how to get somewhere or how to play a game.

Here are Ellie's instructions for making a jam sandwich. The labels show you what Ellie was thinking as she wrote her instructions.

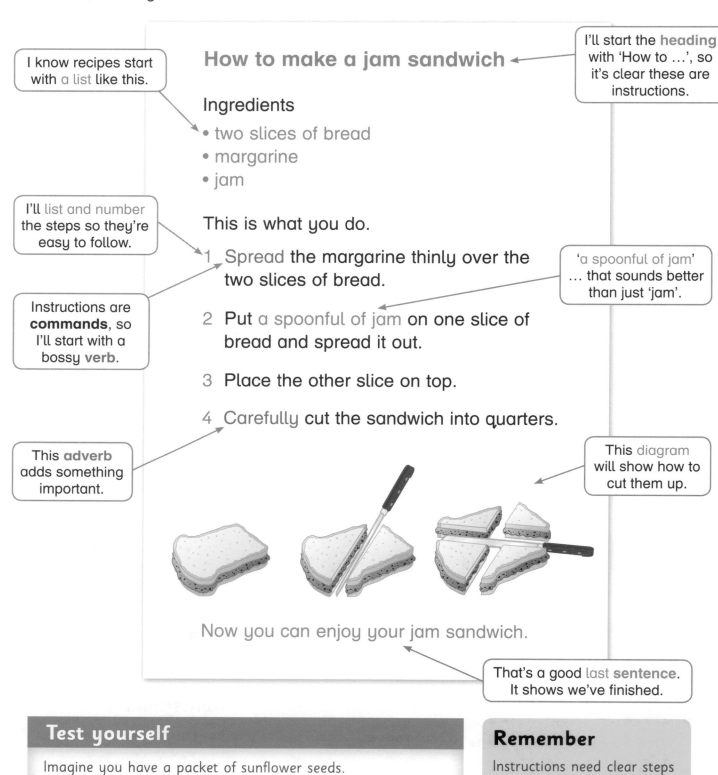

I know recipes start with a list like this.

I'll start the **heading** with 'How to …', so it's clear these are instructions.

How to make a jam sandwich

Ingredients

• two slices of bread
• margarine
• jam

I'll **list** and **number** the steps so they're easy to follow.

This is what you do.

1 Spread the margarine thinly over the two slices of bread.

'a spoonful of jam' … that sounds better than just 'jam'.

Instructions are **commands**, so I'll start with a bossy **verb**.

2 Put a spoonful of jam on one slice of bread and spread it out.

3 Place the other slice on top.

4 Carefully cut the sandwich into quarters.

This **adverb** adds something important.

This diagram will show how to cut them up.

Now you can enjoy your jam sandwich.

That's a good last **sentence**. It shows we've finished.

Test yourself

Imagine you have a packet of sunflower seeds.
Write instructions for how to grow a giant sunflower.

Remember

Instructions need clear steps and bossy verbs.

Writing a letter

There are lots of reasons for writing letters. You can write chatty, **informal** letters to friends to tell them your news. Or you can write **formal** letters to people you do not know, to pass on information or to ask something.

Here is a chatty letter from Abby. She is inviting her friend Leo to a party. The labels show you what Abby was thinking when she wrote each part of the letter.

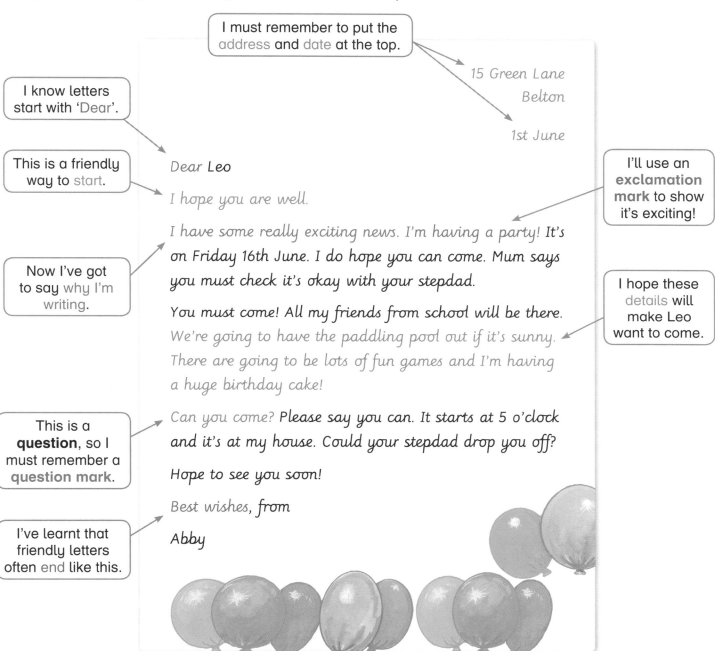

I must remember to put the address and date at the top.

I know letters start with 'Dear'.

This is a friendly way to start.

Now I've got to say why I'm writing.

This is a **question**, so I must remember a **question mark**.

I've learnt that friendly letters often end like this.

I'll use an **exclamation mark** to show it's exciting!

I hope these details will make Leo want to come.

15 Green Lane
Belton
1st June

Dear Leo

I hope you are well.

I have some really exciting news. I'm having a party! It's on Friday 16th June. I do hope you can come. Mum says you must check it's okay with your stepdad.

You must come! All my friends from school will be there. We're going to have the paddling pool out if it's sunny. There are going to be lots of fun games and I'm having a huge birthday cake!

Can you come? Please say you can. It starts at 5 o'clock and it's at my house. Could your stepdad drop you off?

Hope to see you soon!

Best wishes, from

Abby

Test yourself

Write a letter from Goldilocks to Baby Bear, inviting him to her party. Make it sound chatty and friendly.

Remember

Letters can be chatty or formal. You can write different types of letters for different reasons.

Handwriting

Your handwriting is important because you want people to read what you have written. If your writing is not clear, no-one will be able to read it.

Here are some important things to remember when you are writing.

Shapes

Make sure all your letters are the right shape and the right way round. Practise them in similar groups.

c o a d g q   l t i   u y j

r n m h   b k p   v w x z   e s f

Sizes

Keep similar letters the same size. Letters with sticks (**ascenders**) should be taller than other letters.

b d f h k l t

Letters with tails (**descenders**) should go below the line, like this:

g j p q y

Spaces

Always leave spaces between words. Leave a space about the size of a letter, and keep your spaces the same size. Spaces are important.

Itishardtoreadwritingwithnospaces!

Or:

It is hard to read writing with no spaces!

Joins

Start to join some letters if you know how.

ai   at   oi

Test yourself

Write this rhyme in your best handwriting.
Star light, star bright
First star I see tonight.
I wish I may, I wish I might
Have the wish I wish tonight.

Remember

Write clearly. Think about the shape, size and spacing of your letters.

Answers

Page 4
1 Ask an adult to check that you have read the words correctly.

Page 5
1 word → world
2 started → stared
3 place → palace

Page 6
1 delicate – very fine, flimsy, easily torn
2 emerged – came out, appeared

Page 7
1 For example: unkind, unhappy, unpack
2 powerful
3 kindness
4 older

Page 8
4, 1, 5, 3, 2

Page 9
You could have answered yes or no, as long as you gave a reason. But in fact, the answer is no – Bruno has tricked his brother again. This is how the story ends:

But when the next day came, Bruno did not want to go fishing. He was too busy eating fish! And Oscar was too tired to go alone.

Page 10
1 one spring morning
2 He dived around trying to catch fish.
3 under a tree
4 Oscar

Page 11
1 because he had tricked Oscar OR because it was what he wanted Oscar to say
2 because he wanted Oscar to think he was getting tired
3 because he thought there would be more fish the next day
4 because he had done all the fishing the day before

Page 12
1 No, because Oscar was not very clever to fall for his brother's tricks.
2 Here you can answer yes or no. But you must give a reason that mentions something from the story.

Page 13
1 He was a fruit seller.
2 He was kind and helpful because he helped to carry the old man's heavy load.
3 because he cannot reach up to get the best fruit to sell

Page 14
1 that it rains in lots of different places
2 fields, trees, umbrellas, ships at sea
3 'It rains on the umbrellas here,'

Page 15
1 snail and trail
2 that it is slimy
3 any three of these: busy, bee, buzzing, by, buzzily
4 because the zzz sound sounds like a bee OR because it's like busily but with zzz in it

Page 16
1 the dictionary
2 the recipe
3 information about another wild animal

Page 17
1 different sorts of pets
2 sections on different sorts of pets
3 to help us quickly find a word or subject
4 Rabbits

Page 18
1 the young of butterflies
2 so that they grow bigger
3 when they are fully grown

Page 19
1 they are colourful; they are covered with tiny scales; they are 4–6cm across
2 nectar from flowers
3 sucks it up with its long tongue
4 dragonfly

Page 20
Three ideas, for example:
• Rubbish is bad for the environment.
• We need to cut down how much rubbish we throw away.
• We should reuse and recycle more.

Page 21
1 because getting rid of rubbish is bad for the environment OR because we are throwing away useful materials
2 because many people now use recycling bins and there are lots more recycling points

3 because you can put food waste such as vegetable peelings into the compost bin

4 your own idea from the text – for example: taking items to a charity shop OR reusing jars and pots to keep things tidy

Page 22

Make sure each sentence makes sense and has a capital letter and full stop. Here are some examples:

1 I like playing cricket.

2 I threw the ball over there.

3 Put the cards on the table.

Page 23

Make sure each sentence makes sense and has a full stop at the end. Here are some examples:

1 You can wait here or you can wait inside.

2 Jack ran away but the giant ran after him.

3 The phone rang and Mum went to answer it.

Page 24

Make sure each sentence makes sense and has a full stop at the end. Here are some examples:

1 A dictionary is very useful because it helps you spell words.

2 We went to bed when it was dark.

3 The snowman will melt if the sun comes out.

4 He sat on the chair that was broken.

Page 25

Here are some examples:

1 On Saturday afternoon, Dan rode his bike in the park.

2 In the night, Carrie quietly slipped out of the door.

3 The dog ran madly round the garden.

Page 26

Here are some examples of adjectives you might have used:

1 The grand old lady was wearing an enormous blue hat.

2 The big bad wolf climbed the tallest tree.

3 Huge waves crashed on to the jagged rocks.

Page 27

1 The dog barks. The dog barked.

2 He is waiting. He was waiting.

Page 28

We went into the playground. On the grass there was a climbing frame with a rope ladder. Next to it was a sand pit.

Page 29

1 That is amazing!

2 What time is it?

3 Can I help you?

4 Help!

Page 30

On Sunday I went to see my friends Ben and Jacob.

Page 31

1 I had pizza, salad and ice cream for tea.

2 In my team were Alice, Molly, Freddie and Dan.

3 'Stop!' shouted the man.

Page 32

1 can't   it's   I'll

2 I didn't hear Mark's name.

Page 33

1 milk

2 brush

3 clock

4 belt

Page 35

1 fork

2 gate

3 light

4 bowl

Page 36

1 rain-bow   rainbow

2 ca-ter-pil-lar   caterpillar

3 car-di-gan   cardigan

4 hel-i-cop-ter   helicopter

Page 37

Here are some examples of words you might have written:

–et   target, ticket, carpet

–le   bottle, middle, puzzle

–el   camel, level, towel

–tion   section, mention, motion

Page 38

1 chips (or fries)

2 dishes (or plates/bowls)

3 brushes

4 flies

Page 39

1 **a** throwing
   b smiling
   c dropping
   d coming

2 **a** hoped
   b asked
   c tried
   d clapped

Page 40

1 **a** elephant   **d** written
   b knife   **e** mice
   c charge

Page 41

1 any, many
2 most, post/host
3 wild, child/mild
4 there, where

Page 42

Check your spellings against the words in the box.

Page 43

1 I like baked beans.
2 Come over here.
3 I shall wear my coat today.

Page 44

1 hasn't
2 is
3 gave
4 were
5 everywhere

Page 45

Here are some examples of ideas:
Characters: Billy, a wizard
Setting: Billy's house, in a wood
Events: finds potion, drinks it, shrinks

Page 46

Make sure your plan shows what happens in the beginning, middle and end of your story.

Page 47

Here are some examples:
1 All of a sudden there was a puff of smoke.
2 Eventually he reached the top of the beanstalk.
3 The next morning they woke up cold and hungry.

Page 48

Here are some examples of words you might have chosen:
1 The little mouse peered/peeked round the corner.
2 The cake was delicious/yummy/scrumptious.
3 'Please let me go,' begged/pleaded/sobbed the tiny alien.

Page 49

Here is an example of how you might have made it more interesting:
Sammy looked up in surprise when he heard the splash. He stared into the breaking waves. There was something there. It was glinting in the sunlight. It seemed to be made of glass. It was a bottle!

Page 50

1 It was twelve o'clock. Cinderella ran out of the palace.
2 The monster was coming closer. Alex listened for his footsteps.

Page 51

Check your poem:
• Does your poem have a number pattern too?
• Is it written in lines and verses?
• Does it sound like a poem (for example, rhyme or have a beat)?
• Does it use interesting noun phrases?
• Do the lines start with capital letters?

Page 52

Did you think of something for each sort of task?

Page 53

1 For example, you might have added another activity, such as face painting.
2 For example, you might have added insects (such as bees, butterflies, beetles) OR more animals (such as squirrels).

Page 54

Here are some examples:
1 It was really breezy and everything kept blowing over. We even had sand in the sandwiches!
2 It has six legs. Ants live in nests under the ground.
3 They have bright yellow flowers that look like suns. They grow very tall.

Page 55

1 The first flakes of snow began to fall.
2 Fill the flowerpot with compost/soil.
3 Rabbits live in burrows/warrens underground.

Page 56

The question must end with a question mark and the command with a full stop. They should both start with a capital letter. Here are some examples:
1 How are you feeling?
2 Put the books back on the shelf.

Page 57

Check your account:
- Does the first sentence say what special event you are writing about?
- Have you used past tense?
- Are the events in order?
- Have you used linking words or phrases like 'First', 'Next', 'After that'?
- Have you chosen interesting details?
- Have you used adjectives and noun phrases to describe?
- Is there a clear ending?

Page 58

Here is an example of what you might have written:
We built a huge sandcastle and put a flag on top. Then we watched the waves slowly flatten it!

Page 59

Here is an example of what you might have written about birds:
Birds are animals with feathers. They have wings and can fly. There are lots of different sorts of birds like blackbirds, sparrows and thrushes. Lots of birds build nests in trees and bushes but some live in nest boxes.

Page 60

Check your instructions:
- Have you put a heading (for example, 'How to grow a giant sunflower')?
- Have you listed the things needed?
- Do the instructions have clear steps?
- Did you number the steps?
- Have you used commands (for example, 'Water the seeds every day')?
- Have you used noun phrases and adverbs to be clear?
- Is there a clear ending (for example, 'In a few weeks you will have a giant sunflower')?

Page 61

Check your letter:
- Have you put an address and date at the top?
- Have you started: 'Dear Baby Bear' and ended: 'from Goldilocks'?
- Have you told Baby Bear all about the party?
- Have you tried to convince him to come?
- Have you asked questions to sound chatty? Or used an exclamation to sound excited?

Page 62

Ask an adult to check your handwriting.

Glossary

adjective	a describing word that tells you more about a **noun** (for example, a big dog)
adverb	a word that tells you more about a **verb** (for example, the dog barked loudly)
alphabetical order	words put in order using the first letter of each word (for example, ball, goal, pitch)
apostrophe	a **punctuation** mark (') used in short forms (for example, didn't) and with –'s (for example, Joe's dog)
ascender	the long 'stick' on letters like b, d and k
blend	to put sounds together to read a word (for example, c-a-t blends into 'cat')
capital letter	the special form of letter (for example, A B C) used at the start of **sentences** and names (also called upper case letters)
caption	the words that go with a picture, to tell you what it shows
character	someone in a story – a person or animal
comma	a **punctuation** mark (,) that is used to show breaks in a **sentence**
command	a **sentence** that tells you to do something (for example, Stand up.)
compound word	a word made up of two smaller words
consonant	any letter that is not a **vowel**
contents	a list at the front of a book showing what is on each page
descender	the long 'tail' on letters like g, p and y
description	writing that creates a picture of a person, thing or place
dictionary	a book that lists lots of words – it is used to check spellings and might also give the meaning of the words
events	things that happen
exclamation	a short **sentence** that shows surprise
exclamation mark	a **punctuation** mark (!) that is used to show an **exclamation** (for example, Help!)
fact	a piece of information that is true
fiction	writing that is made up, such as a story
flowchart	a diagram that shows a series of **events** in order
formal	language you would use for a serious reason, to someone you do not know
full stop	a **punctuation** mark (.) that is used at the end of a **sentence**
glossary	an **alphabetical** list of the important words in a book, to show their meanings
heading	a title at the top of a page that says what the page is about
homophone	words with the same sound but different meanings (for example, pear and pair)
index	a list of subjects in **alphabetical order** at the back of an information book – it shows the page number next to each subject
informal	language you would use with a friend or family member, to be chatty and friendly
inverted commas	**punctuation** marks (' ') that are used to show when someone is speaking

joining word	a word that links two parts of a **sentence** (for example, and, but, when)
linking word	words that order and link events in a story (for example, later, The next day)
lower case letter	the letters (for example, a, b, c) that are not **capital letters**
non-fiction	writing that is based on **fact** and is not made up
noun	a word that names a person, thing or place (for example, dog, teacher, school)
noun phrase	a **noun** with other words added to it (for example, the big hairy dog)
phoneme	a sound that is used in words (for example, the word 'catch' has three phonemes: c-a-tch)
phrase	a group of words that go together (for example, a pile of boxes)
plural	more than one of something (for example, some dogs)
poet	a person who writes a poem
predict	to say what will happen in the future
prefix	a part of a word added to the start of another word (for example, unhappy)
punctuation	marks that are used to make writing clearer (for example, **full stops, question marks** and **commas**)
question	a **sentence** that asks something or needs a response
question mark	a **punctuation** mark (**?**) that is used at the end of a **question**
report	a piece of **non-fiction** writing that gives **factual** information about a topic
rhyme	words that have the same sound at the end (for example, bin, tin)
rhythm	the beat of words (for example, in a poem)
scan	to look quickly over a **text** looking for a particular word or **phrase**
segment	to break a word into **phonemes** (for example, you segment the word 'sad' into s-a-d)
sentence	a string of words that makes sense on its own and has one main idea
setting	the place where a story takes place
singular	one of something (for example, a dog)
statement	a **sentence** that tells you something
storyboard	a way of showing the main **events** of a story in pictures
sub-heading	a smaller **heading** than the main heading – it says what a section of text is about
suffix	an ending added on to a word (for example, playful)
syllables	the small parts of a word that make separate sounds or beats when you say the word (for example, gar-den has two syllables)
tense	the form of a **verb** that is used to tell you when something happens – present tense is for things happening now and past tense is for things that have already happened (for example, I play [present tense], I played [past tense])
verb	a doing or being word (for example, catch, throw, run, jump, are, have)
voice	a writer's style, which you can hear when you read their writing (for example, chatty, **formal**, descriptive)
vowel	any of the letters a, e, i, o, u